E L E M E N T A L

for maren—
from
Alice B. Fogel

ELEMENTAL

P O E M S
ALICE B. FOGEL

ZOLAND BOOKS • CAMBRIDGE, MASSACHUSETTS

First Edition published in 1993 by
Zoland Books, Inc.
384 Huron Avenue
Cambridge, MA 02138

Some of these poems have been previously published in *A Fine
Madness, Amaranth, Anthology of Magazine Verse and Yearbook of
American Poetry, Boston Review, Connecticut River Review, Crazy
Quilt, Green Mountains Review, Hubbub, Iowa Review, Ironwood,
Minnesota Review, Negative Capability, Passaic County College Anthol-
ogy, Phoenix, Ploughshares, Poetry East, Poetry Northwest, Puckerbrush,
Seneca Review, Southern Poetry Review, Worcester Review, Yankee
Magazine,* and *Zone 3.*

FIRST EDITION

Printed in the United States of America

This book is printed on acid-free paper, and its binding materials
have been chosen for strength and durability.

Library of Congress Cataloging-in-Publication-Data

Fogel, Alice (Alice B.)
     Elemental : Poems / by Alice Fogel. — 1st ed.
        p.   cm.
     ISBN 0-944072-33-X
     I. Title.
   PS3556.0277E44   1993
811'.54—dc20   93-14210
                                                          CIP

FOR MY MOTHER AND MY FATHER,
who gave me life, love, and literature

CONTENTS

E L E M E N T A L

ELEMENTAL

It is never a question of wanting to fall.
It is the precipice which calls, the air
that yearns for the body to caress.
As heaven meets the upward
gaze of earth, and as all land
is water bound, so I am defined by you.
The drowning man pulls up the sea
like bedclothes, and finally is buoyant.
The profiles of the beach — all area
momentarily outlined, then merely memorized:
Once something else, now beautiful. Here
new agates grow unknown, like their aired
ancestors, the arrowheads on drier sand.
Even these stones have always known
where they are going.
They're in no hurry, we don't name them
— or love them — for their descent.
It's elemental.
I'm not talking about the crash.
I mean passion, the wave following
its heart, airborne: No turning back,
no questions asked.

And then,
  to find a way
    outward, to believe
      in opening.
After the long
  quick climb, viney reach,
    offshoot, curtain green,
      to be
a defiant hand,
  offer translucent
    umbrellas
      unspun against the light.
After the sharp
  nipple of bud that pushes
    out hard and
      carefully wrapped,
petulant,
  and thick
    with peaking life,
      to find
the other way, to turn
  outward against the turn,
    the same way a skirt
      unwinds after the twirl:
This is already the end, the dance ended,
  only one moment more, the moment
    of applause; this last
      incidental motion, mere encore.
To open is less a believing than no
  or yes,
    is more a giving up of one will
      to another,
the same as the spiral of pinecone
  that lifts its
    skirts to let fall
      the seeds,

the same as the hailstone
    designed by the flick of wind's wrist
        unwinding
            through insistent air.
Leaf curl, fern furl, curve of lock or twist
    of fate.
        So much planning
           and intent,
so much spent, such a
    time becoming,
        so much of and beautiful this
           briefest blue.

Imperceptible as the motion
of glaciers, the growth
of southern trees
so melts the island
made of ice
loosing itself toward an ocean.
You once lived there, love,
still free, at the Arctic pole,
which lets in the most light.
The wind was moot,
having no object
of affection or aggression.
It was like being on land,
but not like land.
You floated, a world
without an outside world;
wandered, and
conceived of yourself
in a possible future.
It tried to follow you
downstream when you left. It
diminished. Motion of the dim
elements, and radiance,
wore it down.
Now your ice island,
all those years lost,
has been found well
on its way to the Atlantic,
a little glacier dying
for the future. Hard water
riding its shadow,
its friction bears it
out to sea on what it leaves.
As if to say:
I do mean to always love you

but I just can't stay,
each drop will tear
itself away, wanting
to return to itself
any way it can, even by departing.
Willing to surrender
to live forever in another,
it moves toward you
wherever you are,
from under the sodden earth
up into the down of rain.

When I sleep in strange houses and it rains,
I rise up from my bed and stare,
bewildered, out the dark twilled windows.
There's something left out in the rain,
I say, but I can't remember what it is.
Something in my memory rusts or shines
or sinks into the earth,
lost now, but still of great importance.
A baseball glove, a shoe, a book or a tool,
a gift, once upon a time, owned
and forgotten. But more than this,
some ancestral awe of water. Floods.
Lost land. Precarious shelter. The rain
spins off the leaves of trees, the bark,
corners of strangers' homes and barns.
Or slides down the rails and steps
of fire escapes, dark as spears.
The axe? The fenceposts? What?
What is it that worries me, half-recalled
from another life? Something long ago familiar
about the grasses drenched in risen drops,
the sparrows stretching dry their wings,
insects emerging from between cleaned stones —
the ancient rains that made them.
I don't know what it is at the eroding edge of mind
that sticks there like a summer-swollen door;
but the rain stops, and while I sleep,
the wet world evaporates in slow inaudible sighs.

San Juan Island

Everything softens, the rain
makes its slow way
down and through.
You build your house
under water.
No suddenness, no sounds,
as if the hammer
of a gentle man
did to wood the same thing
love does to children.
You sleep
wherever the whim
of night falls,
your comforter the susurrus
talk of drops
too small to see.
In the marsh, sleepy movement
beneath wet leaves.
By the lake, between weeping
willows, the white apples
swell and sway.
For a moment in the mornings
from its pillow
all the blue of the sky
unfolds like a baby's limb,
then settles back
into the same dream,
more soft clouds.

HOPE

It lies in that hollow space
Between the whitish walls of bone
Where blood is made.
One day it travels abroad,
In search of the objective.
You feel it when it dislodges,
A tinnitus deeper than the skull's depth,
The tiniest movement,
As of an eyelash that loosens
And falls past the eye.
Think of our skeletons, oozing marrow:
They look like bamboo
Hung with Spanish moss and spiders' webs
Where hummingbirds might nest.
All else the same — life forces
Turning their usual corners.
A seasonal migration.
Not courage, not a thought
For honor. Just a habit.
Then, hope, in passing
Through some overlooked aperture,
Leaves behind its natural pollution,
Its shadow, the way the sky pulls
Water through its pores.

Life is given
its order: Weather approaches
from a cloudless place
while the past lists
to the other side, more precise
than today.
These are the skies,
full of white paper and lace,
delicate kites of gods on skis.
Life comes down, with its strings,
when the currents of air
can't bear any more.
But the gods don't die,
they occupy themselves in another task:
White flowers bloom on what had seemed
barren trees and grass.
We mistake it for a warm spell
each unaccountable time
the cold stops. Naturally,
things only mean what they are
and not what they may call
to mind. Only — *imagine*:
what they are
is not your cause, but is
because of you.

WHAT TO SAY

Silence is the reward, the word
repeated, droning through the night.
All sound absorbed like color
imploded into white. Silence is the light
touch of life on earth, spilling
across the horizon at sunrise, wanton.
Listen to the snow as it sings
its sentimental story. Listen
to the terrain tell of time and sediment.
Rain remembering land, land forgiving sea;
sea returning to air and salt,
salt stinging the breeze.
I can't explain the fireflies
or the winter's snow or the stone
but I would give them all my tongue
to keep for me, that I might have
something as sound to say.

WHAT BIRDS HEAR

Way above the forests and plains,
forests and plains sculpt space.
That's what birds hear. Air.

So air must be a map,
a geology of silence: It lacks
only the sound of words.

Arctic ice floes are flown by loons in Maine,
and other oceans are shown to teals in waves
of air above the Atlantic.

Now the distant rise and fall of land
announces itself here
in the rhythms of herons in flight.

To birds, the turns and tones of air
are clear geographies
read — like braille — by their wings.

They hear what we can't hear or see —
what we never imagine. Air.
And they sing.

BLUE

"Man worries; God laughs."
Yiddish proverb

Blue is given to nothing
to save it from being invisible.
What is the indiscernible, lovely line
between air and sky?
Real, but as if imaginary,
that moment of blue is the awe-
filled air, sometimes called heaven,
the vanishing point forever
fading out
so as not to seem too sudden.
The unseen and the brilliant there
are one.
Where the future passes on
and spring overtakes the snow,
is all that is known
of the true home of that hue.
There is no one single
glimpse of grace to learn
why, or where, the sky is blue, beyond
the shadow of a doubt.
God lives in that place, laughing.

ALWAYS MOVING

O the intemperate pulse and dance
Of these seasons so in love, moment
To moment moving
Free of holds and wholly held,
Unattached and so a part
Of belonging. Summer's scent unhinged
And set to traveling, sent afar
By wind. Laughter. Listen:
Those nomad moorings, those petalled
Pourings of morning storms: Autumn,
Passionate, impatient,
Is speaking

Of space invisible, divisible, defined
By what is passed, what present.
This is the weather poring over us
In the ecstasy of its unpredictable
Piety. October. November.
What a way to awaken!
Suddenly I know, yes, how it is
That the leaves from sheer beauty
Can dash themselves to earth,
So wonderful in how it moves
Always, in how moving
Is the world.

WINTER

At dawn the snow is falling
Out of its sky
And yet that sky is all
That stays the same. So this
Is how to hide
Even while surrendering!

The Wind Is

The wind is a field, a force
of habit in the world.
No roads, no markers,
no destinations. All it wants

is to travel. By turns it unravels,
a dusty blanket, a freshly peeled
pear left out to dry.

The wind is an heir, a far
cry from home. Given, given.
An indifferent owner. In its carriage

fly the looselimbed, the unnatural
vagabond birds in flight.

I've stood out there waiting: Lift me,
take me, I have somewhere
to go. It passes, passes, listing
east and west, the turning points
of the compass. Listening,

I've heard your sigh across the brightened
miles as if no one
and nothing moved between.

No Less

It was twilight all day.

Sometimes the smallest things weigh us down,
small stones that we can't help
admiring and palming.

Look at the tiny way
this lighter vein got inside.
Look at the heavy gray dome of its sky.

This is no immutable world.
We know less than its atoms, rushing through.

Light, light. Light as air, to them,
for all we know. Trust me on this one,
there is happiness at stake.

Boulder, grain. Planet, dust:
What fills the stones fills us.

I remember, or I have a feeling,
I could be living somewhere with you,
weighted down the way we aren't now.

Often the greatest things,
those you'd think would be the heaviest,
are the very ones that float.

It is that particular moment
when unseen spiders make suppers
on woven plates, moths wake,
clouds celebrate as they go.
Crickets scratch and cheer.

Two small birds almost touch,
and so much space surrounding!
Their tailfeathers wave, swinging
in time, concert violin bows,
to balance on the bough.

How the weeds and tiny trees love to rise
to an occasion. Here, they adorn
an abandoned plow, rusting
into the near edge of the field.
Everywhere

things make their way. Even today
in the low mown grass, stems spawn
yellow or purple flowers, and fur grows
in secret on their leaves. The particles
we breathe sing, passing in and out.

Life, then, and all its details,
will open to the moon, and again, anew,
tomorrow with the sun.
Following the lowering light,
particularly,

my questions ease away,
till the answering echoes return
on the most slender crowns
of the last and longest shadows
of the pines most tall, and farthest west.

How childish to believe that the space
Between earth and stars is filled by only air.

Earth and water are once
Encircled by air, again by fire,
Then by what differs from fire
In its divinity.

Planetary motion inflames the air. All winds

Are not the same wind any more
Than all rivers are but one.

The earth exhales:
Waterdrops ride heavenward upon air,
The breath of condensation.

Mist is residue.

Mountains absorb cool rainfall,
Release it into streams,
Swallow up those
With no recourse to the sea.

Another exhalation:
Minerals and metal, earth's analogies
For haloes and false suns. All metals

Are touched by fire and hold earth, except gold.
All light is touched by water and holds air,
Except the sun.

Rainbows indicate a vision
Weakened by elements.

The yellow is not really there.

LANDSCAPE

Something not meant to fall
Over this earth
Will fall. Sudden veil
Of mourning silk,
Of sorrows and moot
Regret, swallowed by a black mouth
In black waters.

A stillness only known
To mid-ocean
Taking its place on land.

Think of a room,
Now of a dream
In which you are walking
Elsewhere,
Unafraid.
Remember colors.

Forget the terror
White of the whale,
Religious white
Of snow, the annihilating
Nuclear white,
The innocent,
The blinding white in which all colors
Explode at once, like a life
At the moment of death.

As a little girl I thought
I lived in someone
Else's dream.
Waking meant death,
Or change, or loss. Living
Was necessary,

Was the lullaby
Keeping me alive.
The landscape of the sleeping atom
Is in shades
Of shadow, textures
Of ash.
I am not alone here, crowded
Into this world I love,
Smaller
Than a self
Or than a universe
Contained.

GRACE

Hold closely the red, round, sleek,
solid sphere of apple, perfect
in its vulnerability to earth and air.
Inside, seed and flesh
lurk in secret slumber, as if waiting.
But not waiting. Something could grow
out of this, something could burst it apart
from what it seems. Each seed
has a story to tell that it will never tell,
that it hasn't yet lived or learned.

The body is a globe, whole,
contained and fragile.
What it doesn't know is more immense.
You can't surprise it with predictions.
Right now something inside may be swelling,
reaching outward, working
on its own small life.
Maybe one dark seed
snaps open against your fear —
a sudden awakening into night.

You could die of knowing
or of not knowing, or —
smooth the skin against your palm,
slide your nail along its continuous curve,
its utter sheen, while your hand
trembles and dares to go on.
Smell its apple smell of wine
and earth and bowl, get its wet envelope
everywhere in your mouth,
such a dangerous delight.

You have to let in the small wonder
of apple, you have to let please

whatever can please you, hold it
skin to skin, dearly, so the wholeness
of its life passes through yours,
healing as it breaks its way
between the walls of cells.

Untitled

In the heat, crickets go on nattering.
You could take a walk in the rain, hear
Each drop as it touches down.
Or shower, get into bed, watch how dark
The distant hills become when the mist lifts up.

It's true everything is repeated,
Always the same but different each time.
Every move gets worked over, practiced
From another angle. *I want to get this right*,
Things seem to say: All the rain, the night, hill
Upon hill. It's hard to imagine a first time.

Once grass had never felt the crush of wheels,
That sudden downward push to earth.
When it moved, it must have been imperceptibly,
Stretching at first light.
It's something you can't remember
You want to take it all
Into consideration: The innocence, repetition,
Each separate sound on the shingles.

Outside, it's so dark, so silent, it scares you,
Though rain and crickets are throbbing
From everywhere like the growth, in unison,
Of all the world's leaves, or a single
Voice from inside the sky.

NOW AND THEN

Slowly, it is dusk,
Morning,
Spring.
Now you notice, now
Believe in what you see.

You always miss that moment
Of things becoming right; the shift's
No sharper than memory's.
Or maybe nothing
Stirs at all,

But the thing you want to fix
Moves through space — fast,
But still, like starlight.
Imagine that you could trap it once
In a mirror balanced between

Now
And then. The mirror, for a moment,
Holds the two apart,
And holds
The parts together.

DIPPER

If I had lifted my fingers to bead
each star, round and threaded,
onto the weave of evening,
the scene could never have been better.
You were here, and in time
we lost all distinction
between the dark and dark.
The room went inside out.
How your hands rested on me —
that was the way those two stars
balanced on the crossbeam of the window.
These were the base of the dipper,
which seemed to offer our bed a blessing.
The whole cup of the constellation
filled the upper frame.
What was in it and around it were the same,
each familiar to the other
and neither near nor far.
If we leaned, we'd see the handle, pointed west
without suggesting departure.
Distance unfolded dimension, until the four
lit corners of the bowl
were four eyes slowly
circling the globe, while never
losing sight of center.

THE ARCHER

The swaying moon
frees itself scythe-like
from the forest.

When I look to you, the ring
of other nights encircles me
as if from memory

or by heart.
Like the moon, you
step into darkness
                    whole.

I see you lift your bow, hear
delicate feathered arrows shift
in your quiver. This
shot sings with a linear
precision.

The moon falls into me.

SNOWSTORM

There is no sleep
                    in the stillness
of snow, in such
                    an adoration
                              of freefall.
Like a choir's
                    single inhalation, it seems
to pause
                    between two songs. Sleep
slips by me
                    in waiting for the sound.

          Outside
as in the laying down
                              of walls, everywhere
the snow
                    like stone
                              falls into place
and fits, with proper spaces
                                        for the air
to travel.

          You
                    pass through a crystal
greenhouse: angel
                    caretaker
                                        owner
of the key. Lit from within
                                        there
the orchids are in bloom.
                              In my room
when the door opens
                    feathers of snow
                                        fly

into my arms like lovers
                    and disappear.
Then you
          step in
                    from out of the whirled,
lay down with your white bouquet,
breathe the scent of sleep.

The angels are out on Wednesday Hill.
Here, the thousands of Queen Anne's lace
singing with a sound like rain, like yes.
They're rising tall above the field,
nodding — large, then small, until
a mist in the distance.
This is their meadow, their church,
as you are mine, the element
I become, unlaced. Your hands
the hands of the sky.
Those ladies and I —
blithely in the air without wings,
ringing without bells, sailing on high
without seas. . . . For a spell,
the line between this feat and me
flies bright, invisible as pollen:
A life all its own.

THE GARDENER
(After the painting by M. Le Nain, c. 1655)

In standing just beyond her skirts,
in leaning in, and
in that shy lift
of your little finger on the handle
of your hoe — in these we know you.

And she must look up soon,
accept this rose you hold for her.

You leave your eyes on the sure
distance between your finger and the tip
of hers which touches one petal
as if testing it for texture.

One child peers up from under
these splendid hands suspended
like other buds
in all the dark surrounding.

The fall of cloth, the long
pause of women and girls, all
tilt us toward your sweet intent.

Your red coat's sleeve is torn.
She will never mend it, nor mention
what you did today. You will tend
to your garden, she to the table, where
she'll slice the whitest parsnips.

The Bat

Night came over us before the whole sky
had filled in at its fontanel.
Stars turned on near the horizon
like house lights, one by one,
and reckless moths crashed by.
In the valley, fireflies rose
over the old foundation.
The trees you'd tipped
cleared the distance of a darkness
deeper and farther away.

On the edge of the porch you built,
carefully slanted for run-off,
I sat, bare feet touching the dirt
and the wet grass that moved
beneath the night.
I wore the red cotton dress
with little white leaves printed on,
but the red, like the color of the sky,
had no color then. We called it "dark."

You, in cut-offs, stood on the hill
outside the circle of porch light.
We watched the bat, a darker spot
in the dull black air,
its quickness, sometimes,
more perfect than the eye's.
I could see you
but it was the darkness that he saw.
There was no sense in light.

You taught him a game,
throwing a stone straight into the sky
over your head.
He followed it up, arriving first

at the apex, then down, faster
than gravity, missing it on purpose
every time, flying
again and again between the stone
and its direction.

I waited for that thump that would bring
bat, stone, your diversion
down to the earth at my feet.
You never tired, but for me
you were no less distant, no more solid,
than the darkness that was night's
definition. Surely bats know stones
don't fly. So he must have known
you were there — or someone
was there.

CONSPIRACY

I lie awake all night
listening to the dust
murmuring under furniture,
listening for the crack
of light from under closed doors,
hearing the sere heat
in the pipes, the rise and fall
of water in the drains.
There is the sound of my sleep
turning back, taking
all the necessary silence
elsewhere. All night
the brittle bray of logs
in the fire, the high pitch
of their sudden memories
of green.
I listen for the shudder
of window panes
breaking free of splintered frames,
hear the stirrings
among the pillow's feathers
as they try to fly again
and in the curtains closed in vain
against the call of day.
Now the lonely sound
of someone breathing,
a heart beating in my own body,
the nails ripping
out from the fingers
as if they too are leaving
for a better home.

THE SELF, FALLING

That one could be so small, slipping
through its own self, as silt shifts
down through its rock bed. . . .
What happens when we wish
is something unforeseen
and other. That we are drawn
to windows and other openings,
that the threshold is as fragile
as desire. This falling
is a bedtime fable, of finding
bottom, false promise of final
softness there. The rest,
silence. But what is worse
than going on is the ending,
that once there the darkness
silvers the glass to mirror
and the eyes too are open,
horribly. What is that shape
that forms its compulsive shadows
through which it is impossible not, again,
to fall? And still the wishful self
has its own ideas.
That one could be so small
and yet unable to rise, that laws
here are still binding, the legacy
of an ancient alchemy. All that rises
is the voice at the end
of its question, for nothing
weighs more than the falling.

THE LAST NIGHT

My father walking through our house,
setting the picture frames to right.
It is late, and still he does not sleep.
He brushes past the hanging plants
downstairs, the old couch, familiar corners.
My father in the living room,
in the hall, the den, his hands
touching these books and photographs.

Upstairs, standing at the windows,
all the mountains dark. The house
stirs, ashes shift in the raised fireplace,
something falls on the roof. Trees brush
each other, outside, as if to rub their dry
bark smooth. There, where my father
stands on the blue carpet for the last time,
remembering its carpet feel. Here my mother's
glasses rest on the piano, reflecting
a daughter's drawing. Now he memorizes
the simple wood of a shelf, the aging textured
wallpaper, even those things that will go
along with him, losing too their proper home.

Every object, not each one, but all of them.
Not even that, but the life breathing in gasps
throughout the darkened rooms. My father walks,
stands, he closes his eyes and sees, rehearsing
the house like a prayer. This table, this
chair. Those curtains. That door,
the other, closed. My father,
unbelieving before a door, learning how to leave.

BACK HOME

Night is the shadow
of the world; the sky
it falls through — blue,
dark, and wide: What casts
shadow colors that shadow
after itself. That day
I only noticed how the light
encircled the sidewalk below.
And the way the tree by the window
was suddenly green, and how
the robins sang there that morning
so furiously full of joy
that I could hardly hear his voice
breaking, on the phone.
The white dogwood sending scent,
the garden patch begging
for seed, the magnolias heavy
with spring. The day my sweet
mother tried to die.
It was April, too much blooming
to bear, too many insufferable seasons,
birthdays, and more work to be done.
Another day to rise to,
another day of lies.
Last spring I saw her hold up the dark
soil in her two hands like a mother,
and when she said how beautiful,
his indifference fell on her like pain.
It was the same as hers for him.
My father knows as well as I
the way time does its work,
what is material, and what passes
for the living, for the left.
That a simple word or deed
can irrevocably affect, that errors

and sorrows choke like weeds.
What follows is what we're left with now,
knowing more of loss, and feeling how
much more of life's to live.
There are those we love but are unable
to see or hold. It's not we
that keep them alive, and thank God,
for we are imperfect, and we forget.
And yet it's in us to give more.
Each tone, each touch, leaves
its imprint, like the children's muddy shoes
on the carpet, or a body so many years
upon the marriage bed.
This was one more sad deep sleep,
but meant to last; his waking her
one new moment of saving grace.
That threshold between the rooms
of living and death is the greatest of all
fine lines. He lifted her in his arms
and carried her back home.

STILL LIFE

All that you have wanted comes to you
as apparitions, accusing
you of not wanting them enough,
knowing you knew how. They wander
wilsome as scales and arpeggios
unsucceeded by sonata. Love,

what is love but a concentration
and who knows better
all that is given to be loved? How can I
be telling you? You: teacher, elder,
my father. You could forget

yourself in return for all that's offered
for memory. So take care of that old man
you have not yet become:
He is the only child who will prove you.
Now, get up, don't grieve. After all,
it's still life. I tell you, the sheer

weightlessness of a tree's branch is in its reaching
for the distances, for all the world
like the curve of earth.
You can feel how the lune of its embrace
includes you, when you look out to sea
and know the horizon

is only a line the mind draws
for comfort.

Here is the proof
of what's impossible to know:
Our parents when younger than we,
and ourselves when older than they.
You can barely touch it
without the black velvet pages,
heavy as handfuls of loam,
turning to weightless dust.

Here's the ship, with crowds of men, clouds
arranged about the masthead.
Friends with names like Newt and Chazz
pose with Japanese girls.
My father leans in close, holds a puppy
named after himself. Artful shots
of miniature bridge over stream,
curve of snow, fountain.

I read my father through his past,
which is my past. I use his eyes
then, in the future now:
That's the gift.
I enter through them, here, in this album
of focused views and clear wonder,
of certain youth, and an age
born old already from the human heart.

You can see how the children love him,
two bundled boys by a lamp-post,
a girl holding a smaller one, too shy to look.
They too speak with their eyes.
Here's a fish-market octopus, here a woman

kneeling by her baskets on the walk.
Rickshaw, thatched roof, baseball game.
Ruined building, bonsai, Russian troops.

Here are the modern streets of Tokyo,
a bride in traditional dress.
Here the farms at Akibane,
a "prize-winning" still life silhouette.
This is how they build with paper and wood.
This is how a young man — a boy —
his first time away from home —
sees his future back there.

When I see what he saw, I can almost believe
what the physicists say: That time moves
in both directions at once. Maybe it's true
that I'll grow old in the future, and wonder
about the past instead. Maybe it's true
that my father is no longer young with new
and watching eyes. Maybe I was always there
waiting to be looking back.

GRACE

Consider the awkward stance
of the stationary object
disappearing behind its paralysis,
etching all the air around
into visibility.

The flying know the open
spaces between things. Faith
in flight, the swallows
darting through trees
as if matter were only imaginable.

One morning the dragonflies,
fleet of tiny winged horses
weaving in from sea like a second sky,
parted around me as if I
were something that had always been

standing by this ocean on this day
and on all the days of their folklore
as they flew past me, always
on their way to grace.

THE EMBRACE

When you had gone I witnessed the breaking
of summer trees, they were breaking
through their own bark, in order to bloom.
Then they did bloom, as before, again.
Our eyes open at the exact moment
of loss. Eyes full of calm,
no matter what, eyes calmly filling
with tears as if tears
were the same as blessing, the same
as sorrow when lulled to sleep
on a slow caress. Sorrow hushed by a voice,
your voice, personification of wind,
wind turning nimbly around the imaginary
and the hard lines, pure air responding to touch
with words. Words, air, reason,
only the names of things uttered.
You wanted to know how it might have been:
It has already happened, will happen.
According to the spherical occurrence
of time where we live among the blooming and breaking
of trees, everything has already been
taken care of. The current that runs through us
is not linear, it is a curved line, carefully
curling back upon itself
in one long unbroken embrace.

Of the Heart

In the heart, we expect to meet
what is waited for around corners.
And what we leave behind
is still ahead, like the sailor's home
as he sails around the world.

The heart is a mirror, you said.
In it we know what can't be known
with any other part of the body.

I see the evergreens following you
up beyond the timberline.
Together you climb
on to where the horizon
blends with all the rest.

Down below, entire landscapes move
with the indifference of passersby.
Marsh becomes meadow, mountains bloom
into breeze. Those trees
run about the hills like antelope!

The sky is shining like silvered glass.
I see you in it, and know.

COME TO LIGHT

All summer my hands strengthening
from good tools in wood —
a texture that gives in, resists, and gives.
All year the changing, mostly the trees',
the milky sap squeezed out beneath a chisel
slicing across seasons once spun
through trees now turning
into posts and beams.

The living, the still-growing trees,
and sometimes a secret dark moon —
the dense root of a branch
begun here — knotted so deep
within, so long ago, that I am ashamed
to have revealed it. How I worked carefully
around the whorl, but firmly.
How I thought those times of what radiates
from such a particular, invisible center.

The trees, the wood, the home we are making,
the green and gold still wheeling
around the heart. This day
when the slow work of years and days
was raised upright like a forest or a house
of prayer, and held together,
surprising and true.

And I want to remember the air
alive like this with leaves, a threnody
of other trees ringing their leaves
through clear September air;
and our hewn hemlock, perfectly joined,
rising through the wild-wind colors
of the best and brightest and saddest season,

and the whole horizon opened up and calling
from the mountains to the rafters.

When there was a little rain,
and a little sun, and later a slight
and sickle moon that rose up high through the purlins
as if to cut clean the ribbons of grain,
as if the changing weather might scrub and shine
the bones of a home that lives
beneath the blessing sky.

How It Ends

Tonight the air is heavy; its moisture
holds its own light, visible as stars
in the slender branches of trees.

The sad grass thickens with it,
welcoming water one last time.

It's as if the air believes
it can absorb gravity, and hover,
never arriving, never leaving.
As if breathing

the scent of fog on the fields
could be enough
for all growing things to forget
the odor of their own decay.

Still it doesn't rain; this air
is like a promontory, is like a body
folded in upon itself, afraid.
A promise awaiting fulfillment.

The air, lost in its intent, holds still,
full of what it will not give.

This is how it all ends: Morning
will burn it off. Winter will set in.

WINTERING

When it comes breaking the sky
in two, I hear it first
and face the wind to wait.
I squint past where eyesight fails,
rooted to the ground in winter
seedlings of rye,
tasting the crisp and sunshot
apple-cold air — and there —
the line of geese
appears, waving like heat
leaving for the south.
Last night six deer met in the yard,
two of them too small for wintering.
Maybe strewn fruit and cabbage stems
give them some animal equivalent
of hope. They must know,
the way that these things know,
that this is the season to die.
But then death
always travels alongside us,
close as peripheral vision.
There are ways of living
through these days of dark and cold.
Go underground, build shelter, trust
in windfall. Look out for the horizon
spinning south like geese,
for that glassy yellow light,
for frost embalming the grass.
Wait, slowly, and stay in this world
with me,
searching the distance for a way
to live in place
of giving in.

THE HOE

In March the earth breaks open, stirs
from its suspension: Water
puddles and floods
our road. You take your hoe
when we go walking, and you fold
soaked earth into soft pleats,
to let the water flow. You free
the orphaned pools to travel and rejoin
their brooks and streams,
and the braided water leaps
between new wet walls, and falls
over the edges of road
and into woods.
With your hoe you scoop
sodden leaves into woven walls, so
these floodgates open, this drawbridge unlocks,
these little excesses of ice and rain and snow
run off, without turning back.
I stay, and watch you clear our way,
parting mud with sure true strokes,
leading water to where it wanted to go.

WHERE WE STAND

Here where the snow came to light
to rest, we stand
listening for the peas now
pearling in their boats.
Here where the birds dove
and swam through the piled snow,
new seedlings are growing
up and through.
The most fragile line of green
heaves aside the rocks and earth.
Make way. Tiny veins are filling.
Tiny vines unfurl. Drops of water curl
into pockets and contours of soil
coiled and braided by worms.
We stand here beside this garden.
How small we are, we whisper.
We grow smaller all year long.
What is beneath us is never
smaller than ourselves.
History; seedlings; even heat
will rise. You and I — we too —
are rooted here, loving
to watch it happen.
We can wait.
We have the time.
What is planted well will come to light.

HOW TO LIVE

In the northern plains grass grows only
for the reindeer. The grass gives
them strength enough to live
till invisible flies come
and run them to their deaths.

At war, soldiers cease
to reason, but differently
from the dancers and the mountain
climbers whose bodies
know what freedom is.

Love is as semaphoric.

All things are of two
natures. For identification,
one remains with the body, held
for safekeeping. The second
is for the living, for the knowing

how to live
without knowing how.

Walking through the Ice Storm

I'll admit I was scared,
but not of falling
on the frozen road. It was you
who mostly missed the ground.
If I held on to you
it was not from fear
but so you'd have something
to stay for, to believe in.
I listened to the bitter air
hissing, flinging its blistered
beads, sharp as syllables:
Luck. Fate. Bullets.
A sky of ice fell over
everything we said, encased it
in glass caskets. I said
you use your loneliness to wound me.
You said your kindness
poisons me. I felt the sky
cut into slender nails
slipping through my skin.
I heard the cold November trees
grieving like hooded widows.
I saw you gliding beside me
like the ghost not yet
cold enough for this storm
to bury.

Let him walk.

Though he knows nothing of it,
it's the one thing he does with ease.
So I keep myself
from calling out his name.

He doesn't see me, awake, beside him —
but I, like the true sleepwalker,
follow after him, out of doors,
over the rails, out into the danger

zones. Night after night, unafraid,
he goes looking; and I watch,
in order to be the one
who will remember.

He never knows why —
like the dancing princess who every night
wore out her newest shoes —
for him the mornings have no rest.

This is his other life,
the one he's never dreamed of,
in which he dares the darkness
and defies all heights.

I hold my breath
while he walks the precipice
with the acuity of the blessed.
They say

if you wake the sleepwalker,
he may fall; but sleeping,
he forgets he ever climbed at all.

It's hard to tell
that the face of the moon
is as much like a man's
as god's. Out yonder,
in the world without us,
who's to say? —
Either we get in the way,
or things make use of us.

Half-way around the globe
from where they started,
the static sound of starlings
echoes off the barn roof.
Spiders weave in the spokes
of wheels, and stars
circle unsuspecting suns.
Little do we know,
the world has a talent
for making itself at home.

Meanwhile, we paint our self-
portraits on everything
imaginable, then hold
them up like mirrors.
Our mercurial brushes
grow longer, our skills
more acute. Dust clouds
the vision, tinder
to the eye. So we burn
trees to save the forests, burn
air to fly afar. We do, we say.
We can. The time

is close at hand. Time was
(said a man)

you could tell the weather from the moon.
That was before another
broke the quicksilver distance
and walked all over it.
Now you can't tell a thing.

LESSON IN PHYSICS

Notice how snow is both one and all:
Every one hides, while all surrender.
I envy this talent for wedding
Love with self-defense.

Although the distance from the given
Here to there is forever
Divisible by two, what we aren't told
Is that parallel lines *will* meet —
Meaning they become one.

This is the physics of infinity:
It is a specific place,
Knot of many nothings, final
Matrix of arcs and grace.

Lullaby

You lay stones over the burial earth
to keep the body from returning
the way it returns, a terrible
rebirth, in your dreams.

You had to do it yourself:
Dig the hole, wrap your dog in a blanket,
lay him down and shoot him.
Later, he's back again, curled at your feet,
autumn red and brittle
as old leaves.

It's the mind's devotion to the familiar
that resurrects, makes a mantra
of love-borne pain.

                    You see
the same remembrance draping
the infant's eyes with their ancient sadness.
It's just like yours.
When he learns how to speak of it
he too will have forgotten
reasons to explain.

What is asked of us includes
the unasked questions of the mute,
imagined and translated only
by someone like you.
Full of the newly lost and newly gained,
you stay awake at night engraving
their inarticulate speech on your heart.

Now when our son cries you lift him and then
bed him down, swaddled and rocked,

somewhere warm beneath the weather.
Return him to earth from his unleashed dreams,

cradled and rocked, cradled and rocked,
then come back to bed, let me hold you.
Sleep.

If I Sleep While My Baby Sleeps

I will hear his sleep
in and through my own, my sleep
will be bathed in his as if we slept
in one same fluid

My sleep floats within a listening
so deep that the separating
spaces of air become
as pliant and full as snowfall,
its singing silence as profound

My ears and his throat —
the sensation of anticipated
hearing close inside the ear
and the incipient murmur or cry
forming at the end of his sleep —
borne like birds and thrumming
on the air of rooms between us

My own sleep will be his
clock, safely keeping time,
his sleep tunes my dreams to listen,
our sleep binds the hour,
heavy and warm,
into a blanket of air
and sound

Shape first, and texture, the juncture
of color, light and dark:
glass panes reflecting sunlight,
the wet deck deeply shining
with darkened day and distant trees.
Jake's new eyes open outward,
ever farther into our world.
Bodies move through rooms.
Up in the skylights leaves explode
from summer into fall,
and through the glass doors
the mullioned landscape
reads like his nine-square quilt.
Patterns bloom everywhere,
rising from floors and furniture.
Outside, tree trunks crisscross in syncopation
beside the road and through the woods.
Dimension telescopes, turns inside out:
a hanging cube flattens against the wall,
patchwork flowers leap for the hand.
At night stars crowd the eyes,
close overhead like a hood.
Dawn comes candystriped, and the sun
cuts the horizon like a baby's tooth.
Will the phantom things — running water,
shadows of hands, the ceiling fan
sweeping in silence —
become unstrange, unwonderful?
Dust motes in sunbeams, water standing
in cut glass, the eye-like knots
in pine boards of ceilings and floors —
everything alive, everything sensible
with life, shape, and light
bright as noise. The air shimmering
vivid as flesh. Negative space

pulsing at its borders. The active shine
in his own eyes meeting eyes
sentient with awe in the mirror.

THE WHITE AND FROZEN PLACE

So much snow falling becomes
One snowfall, one winter, lengthening

The shadows of things caught
In a day's last light.

Even the dead trees
By some trick of light
Seem to grow once more.

So much room

Between the four winds crossing one another
Like familiar enemies.

So much frost and forgetting
Where the heart is.

Under a halo of woodsmoke

Someone adds dry twigs to a fire
Designed to melt the dense season, inseparable
From the lost heart.

Someone, maybe,
Who knows about breaking ice floes, the silence
Of new growing things,

And the sudden recognition
Of once forgotten footprints.

It is a long walk back
Over such deep snow, such a white and frozen place.

FIREFLIES

It had to do with light.
It had to do with open doors,
with darkness and motion, with light.

A dark road, unpaved,
and just us walking to a meadow
opening from trees, an expanse

that in memory fills the world,
crowds trees and homes
so far into the edges
that they become merely frame.

The field was dark but not alone;
it was full, and moving.
It moved upward, it pulled me upward,
drew the grasses upward,

into the bottomless skies.
Fireflies — shadowless —
lifting the air on blinking wings,

rising, with each flash streaking
the whole earth upward
in light brush strokes. We saw

the earth rising like dust motes, unearthly,
the sky rising like starlight,
skyward. We collided there

with the light and silence
exploding the air,
uprooting trees and grasses and heaving earth.

In that moment I regretted our unlived lives,

sad moons eclipsed,
and I saw through them,
darkness lit from the inside.

He wants to build stone walls with his father.
He wants to reconstruct the legacy of old stones,
clear the land and weight it down
around its edges. He wants to take in hand
the cool rough bark of rock, soothe it
in uplifted palms.
He wants to lift the heaviest ones,
to learn the feel of balance and the heft of space.
He wants to place the stones one by one
in a structure of rows where one won't count,
so that the strength of number holds,
and leans in on itself. He wants to pass the stones
in silence, hand to hand, in agreement
with their perfect fit.
He wants to work the stones just so,
to make a thousand framed keyholes of air.
He wants to build the hard, silent, heavy
walls of stone around a common land,
letting each stone linger in an open hand,
unique and familiar as home.

Balance

Balance is everything, is the only
way to hold on.
I've weighed the alternatives, the hold
as harbor: It isn't safe
to let go. But consider the hover,

choices made, the moment
between later and too late.
Hesitation is later, regret
too late. You can't keep turning
and turning, or expecting
to return. This earth

is not a wheel, it is a rock
that erodes, mountain by mountain.
And I have been too soft,
like sandstone, but there is a point
where I stand without a story,
immutable and moved, solid
as a breath in winter air.

I have seen my death and I know
it is my neighbor, my brother,
my keeper. In my life
I am going to keep trying
for the balance,

remembering the risks and the value
of extremes, and that experience
teaches the length of allowable lean;
that it is easier — and wiser —
to balance a stone as if on one toe
though it weigh a hundred pounds

than to push it back against the curve
of its own world.